Ruby in the Rough

Ruby in the Rough

A dedication to **LaToya Ruby Frazier**

Created by:

Shea Cobb and Amber N. Hasan

ISBN: 978-0-578-57842-2

DEDICATED TO

LATOYA RUBY FRAZIER

Edited and Designed by: TuKlor

Printed in United States of America

CONTENTS

RUBY in the ROUGH

Trust is everything these days as an artist, it's my biggest challenge. The phone call that lead me to LaToya came from a trusted source, my sister and friend Amber Hasan. She said "sis you feel it out and see". When i met LaToya, and saw she truly cared about her own causes and not the causes of the media, trust established itself between us.

Latoya is a true guiding light for me. She answers when she can. She sacrifices for her faith in creativity. She is a warrior. Sis, I'm honored to have you so close to me. For your mind and heart and power to express justice in an unjust world.

Watching you set up shot after shot is to see what passion looks like. I take that inspiration and write read and encourage myself to stay in the fight. I have soared spiritually with our sisterhood. I'll continue to soar because you're so Fli-city-fly! My heart is always warm and inspired by your gift of giving. It teaches me to receive. It teaches me to love. It takes my anxiety and builds trust. You trusted me to show you flint. I showed you my family and you became family. You always got flint, cuz you got me and all of us always and forever. I love you. Thank you for changing my life.

Shea S. Cobb

"Phire"

There are some people who feel like truth when you meet them. LaToya is one of those people. She is genuine and honest from the moment you encounter her. I had no intention on liking or trusting LaToya. She was working with a big name magazine and I felt that there was a possibility that the editorial piece that she was involved in creating may have been a way for the magazine to opportunistically exploit to Flint Water Crisis for their own gain. After one meeting with LaToya, I was at ease. Only an artist with her passion and commitment to sharing people's real stories could have convinced me to participate in the article in anyway, I am a chronic skeptic!

LaToya soon became family. She is now part of our sisterhood, a sovereign space where we share and support one another. LaToya has shown me that she loves me and believes in my abilities as an artist.

My art is how I communicate, it is how I convey my emotions to the world around me. This book is truly a labor of love and appreciation for LaToya, and not only for her art, but also for her integrity as a human being. LaToya is real and consistent, so I hope that she accepts this humble gesture of our appreciation for all of the beautiful truth that she captures and shares with the world.

Amber Hasan

"Loud Mouth Ghetto Girl"

1 PART ONE

With every step toward the unknown your love grows
outside its comfort zone
We included
Time is useless

We were born of the same stone
Cut in the same spots
Healed from the same rocks
Mine from Flint
Yours from Braddock
Sisterhood is the by product
When my body broke in rashes
    Our children facing ashes and rotten pipes

Questions without answers

    I don't know why people are bad
But some angels come with cameras
And compassion for the masses
And to meet one,
is to see how people are good.

As is the creator
Same thing really

    Black girl magic captured
You feel like sister
    Like sunshine
I had no plans in trusting you

But your truth tore down walls
And left a foyer
Full of art and anointing

A place of worship in its purest sense
No schedules or B selections
Just beings, being human
Members of the same tribe
Singing the same song
Dancing the same drum
Warring with the same tongue

I can ride peacefully now.

Sisters you count on like multiplication
The love aggressively expands
my hands can't always hold it all
Thank God for you
True blue in brown skin sista
Tearing down them old houses
With a shimmy and a click
Who's juke joint is this?

Hers!

Mine
Ours
Theirs
Our music plays loud
We dance Sabar
And in that moment
We understand that we are sacred

I pray that we can reference that understanding
During those times when we feel vacant
When confidence is latent
I pray we be patient with ourselves

We’re sisters
And that's what sisters do
Constantly remind a sister
That she's beautiful
And worth time, hell that's why God made time
For every moment to be full of efforts
And mistakes
And falls
Enough opportunity to show us whether we walk or crawl
Eventually we will fly
On the wings of sister voices
Gliding with our choices and cheering us on when thinking becomes overrated
Life givers as the ancients have tested
We gone make it

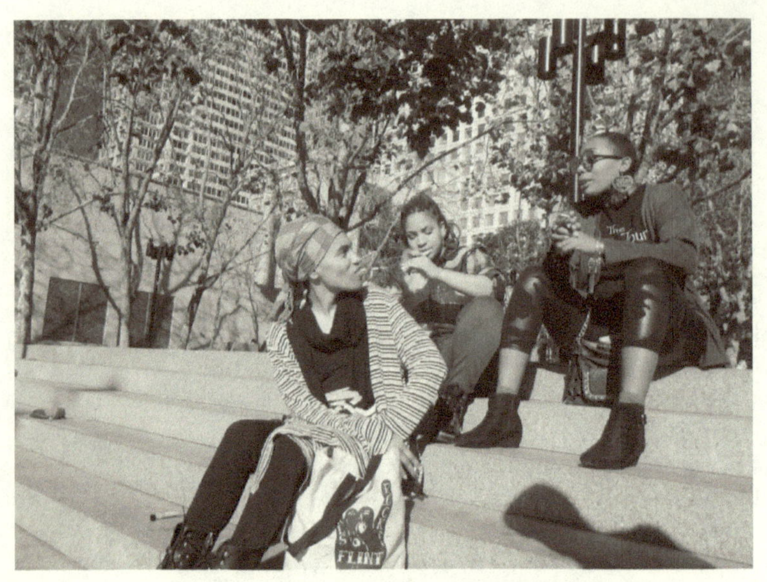

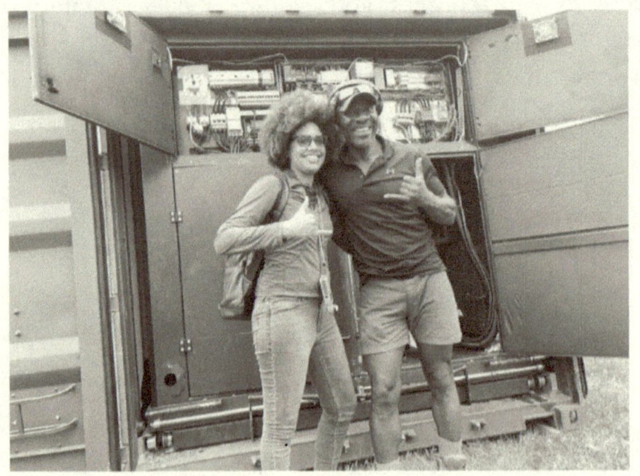

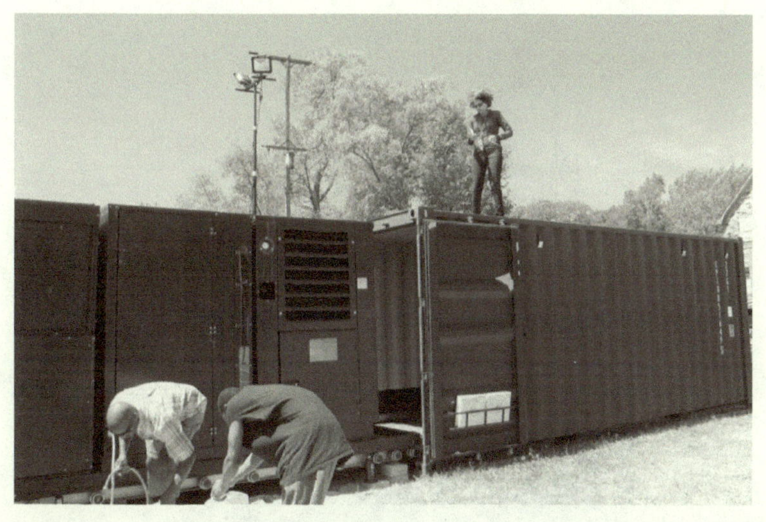

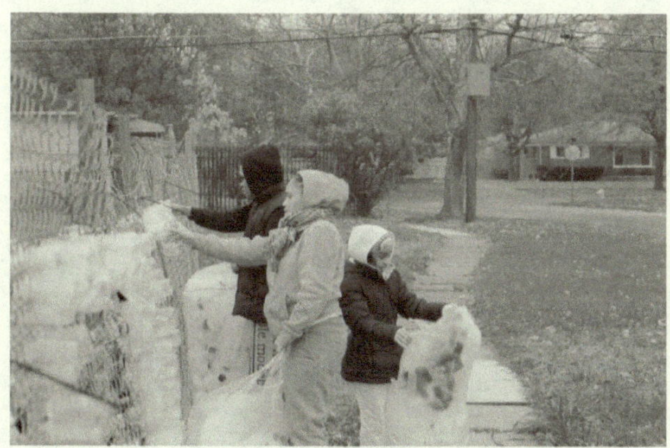

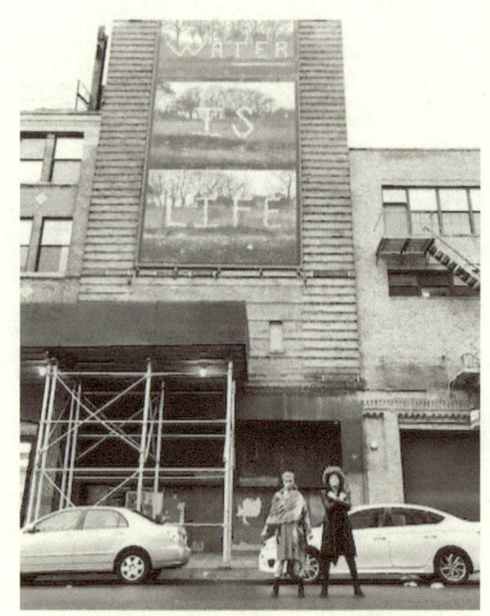
WATER
IS
LIFE

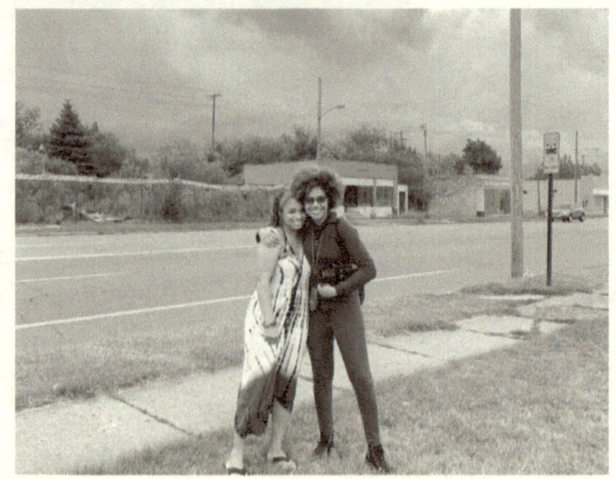

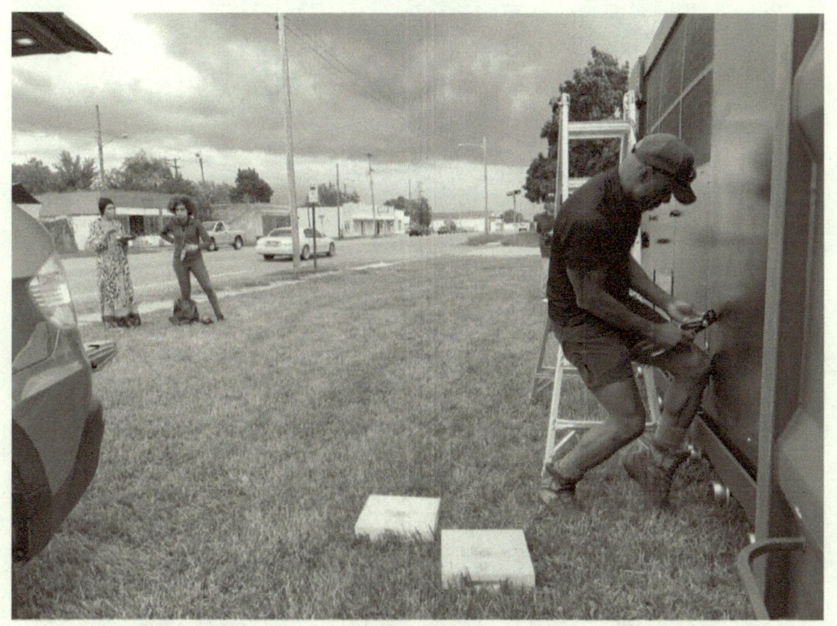

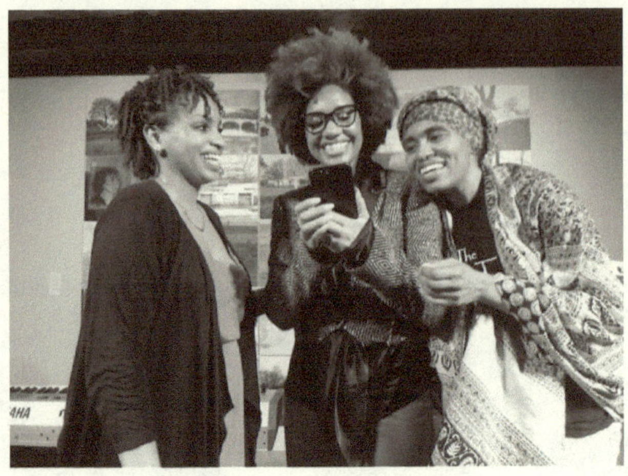

The
SISTER
Tour™

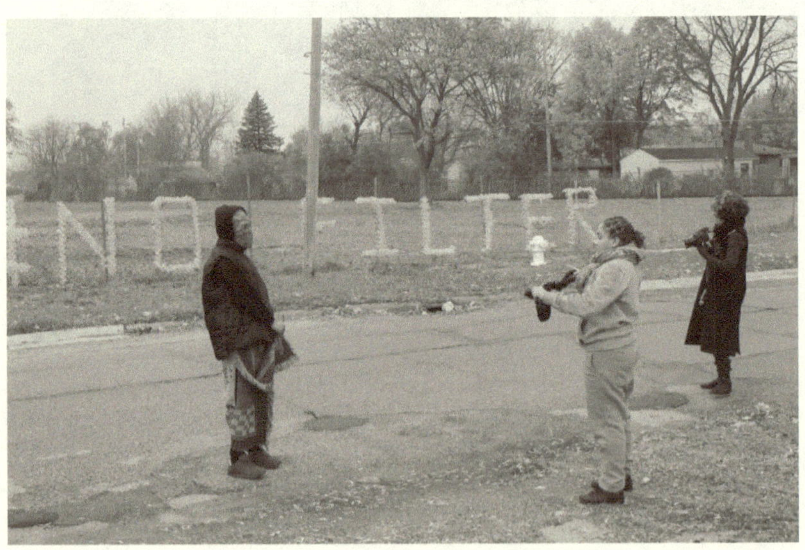

2 PART TWO

It is always the big things that we take in vain
Not realizing the importance until we're feeling pain

It is always the little things that we take in vein
Shoot it into our existence until nothing but little things remain

Why do we complain?

Why must we restrain?

How do we maintain?

Quite Simple…

Sunshine and Summer rain

Arms out stretched with smiles to the sky

Thankful is the spirit
Grateful is the life

Who was I before this moment of clarity?

What was I looking at before?

Did I really see?

I was so blind trying to discover if there were any people like me
No idea I had to accept love from so far a hand

Till I saw you stand the same stance in the sunshine and summer rain.

Remember your youth
And call it good

Not naive or stupid

Because in truth your youth is the very best version of you
And how crazy is it
To let the experiences we face
Take away healthy perception of self
Let's revolutionize the world then and remind them of who they can be
By being who we are

National,

local,
famous family stars

Born to keep close the recipes of love, friendship, and good wine.
Take flight with me and whisper through every poem, and every picture
The keys to unlock the forgotten souls of youth

So we can stop losing to a world of fickle adults
Who question everything but pray for answers
Waiting on salvation
Vanity makes them think that they are chosen

So they wait

Frozen by fear of failure and a lack of faith in their own fight
Lack of faith in their own light
Afraid of their own darkness
But will dwell in it out of spite
Will save face before saving a life

So we prepare swords and pens
it's either kill or write

"I ain't no killa but don't push me"
You don't know my power, the whole world came from black Pussy
Every pulse and pulsation
Every rhythm and vibration

Every drop of sustenance and libation
Mothers of creation

We make miracles

Manifestations of love
Wearing our big girl pants
And Our Ruby slippers
There is no place like home
Even when it hates you
Click dem heels Dorothy
Ease on down that road
be bold
Fuck tornados
Be the tornado
Keep spinning
Keep swimming
Make waves
Mami Wata
Blame it on the rain
Cry me a river
And keep it moving
The struggle don't care nothing about the weary
A black girl's mantra
Cuantos en mi contra
Realmenta no importa
Meantras tenga a mis hermana

We are a force, navigating our way to the source
Lighting and paving the way for one another

3 PART THREE

Whether our hair be straight, kinky, curly

It's ours!

We make it good
We make it against all odds

For every commercial that flags our bounce
Attempting to force us out of every picture
As if we were mere chalk drawings on the sidewalk
Beautiful enough to be magic
Frail enough to just wash away
I wish a MF would try to play me
Like I'm some tragic story ended by colored water

I landed in Flint
I landed in Braddock
I landed in woman
Which is Fine
Considering it's where we're all from
A frequency out of this world
And beyond

Check your imagination
Check your ego
Check your currents

As artists we are servants

Even if only to ourselves
Unveiled
  unapologetically black

Henrietta Lacks
We be HeLa's
Healers
They sell us on a cellular level
Can only digest us in small doses
To potent
Can't stomach our stew
Can't season that brew like our grandmothers do
Bruja bitches
Weaving lessons into our switches
Love so relentless
Seems as if it's endless
The secret is that it is
We are it's womb
It's rib
Where it lives
We house humanity and look at the thanks we get
Unsung

We walk like warriors
Full of elegance and combat
These are the best life has to offer
These select few
Each chose and were chosen to escort my soul
For safe passage
To promise and purpose
By power, divinity, passion, beauty, intellect, unity, and intuition

Brave like elders and ancients
Who see what I haven't
Fearless like children
Patient for maturity because they rushed it before

Wise women walk those burning sands
Giving from that wisdom
And teaching from experience
How am I even here if not for them?
Securing the lines through the storm

Even if it meant
Hoisting them

They say, "sometimes is better to see how the wind carries you so you know what it feels like to be free"
To be one with the elements is to accept them when your control is threatened

You have to respect them
Like they do when the sun is bright
And the sky is blue
And for the first time
I get it
The best way to live life
Is to live it
And i realize i walk among them
We all follow each other
In some way or another
Making the choice to be
Better for me
Cuz i look up to my sister's.
I am my sister's
We keep currents in high tide
Hydro electric femininity
Smiling in wholeness
With poetry to help us learn
That we're better than we were yesterday

4 PART FOUR

We give a fuck

And that's what they fear

We are ferocious and fragile

Fully feminine, whatever that might mean

However that might manifest

We are love in the flesh

Which looks like work to the untrained eye

We look like puzzles before you find the corner pieces

We are the keepers of secrets

There in lies our sanctuary and our struggle

Choosing what to funnel and when to muzzle

Oh Rapunzel your afro is flat on one side

She inspires

Built for the storm
She drags on the lessons most put down
Determined to learn
Fuck the curve
You handle those with speed once you get in em
Like her,
but most slow down so the wind is missing from their kite.
She's expected to provide the tornados
Tame them, and save those who could be destroyed.
Blow winds blow
Breathing fires deep to stoe
For a rainy time
When those flames will fuel her balloon

And maybe that balloon will take her home
I hear there's no place like it
I also hear that it isn't really a place at all
It is a feeling
A knowing
A kneeling
where you meet your maker
In all of your murkines

Home is where your humility is
It's where everybody knows you name but they still call you pookie anyway
Because to them you will always be who you have always been
No growing up in Neverland
Your people will never let you off the hook

5 PART FIVE

I was born by a river
In a broken city
The product of the infidelity of industrialization
Fuck em til they come without you sending for them
Be the North star
Build your factories along the underground railroad
They wade in the water waiting for God to trouble it so rape the rivers too
Say that it's prophecy come true
When the moon shines on me
And I'm reminded of how much I need just a little light to be a guide
Don't need the whole thing
Worry hits my house about demolition of the property
Not because it's worthless, because I want it
I grew up there, and they're trying to take it
Hatred stands off with my love
So I balance the air
And take in the night times we share
For there's nothing better than time with you
Nothing more valuable than laughing at present
Regardless how blue
Nothing bigger than your afro
Your dignity, your fight, your freedom
You added to what it means for me to be a woman
For that I'm proud of you.
Can't always look at the first lady cuz she don't look like me
And I ain't posed for no nudes,
guess I'm not for seventeens president elect
I am however for every she
That guiding light
That shines on me
Reminds me of good ole moon shine.
Elixir of the elders

Take a shot and share a bit with
Eshu and Shango and Oshun

  Shelter of sisters

We build homes in our hearts
  Stay as long as you please, just don't make a mess
I am but breath surrounded by flesh and spirit

Sacred balance

We walk in it and fight for it
Ask
  Ng Mui
We are the origin
and revelation
From the lineage of Lucy

Name means light
  it is what we are even in our shadows
Even in our shallows
  beaming from our marrow

I am but dust without you
Life giver, black healer

The mirror that I'm privileged to see the real me in,
So I can be brave,
take on the waves,
  and face off with the troubles of today.

The problems I face are just thoughts and what are those but subject to us?

We can think this through

So away with the old,
  create new.

I learn from you how to be like God

Thick curly hair and earth skin
Sun filled eyes and multiple shutter speeds

I have an image, I have a wisdom
In you I have a sister
Not bound by religion
What is it without cut outs of clones?
We are different because we're born specific, and that's to eternity as us is to friends. We blend.

Like pixels

we are all but small pieces of creation
suspended animation
Imitation is the greatest form of flattery
I hope that The creator appreciates the gesture

That same girl that strip
Is the same CEO of a fortune five hundred company
The same hoe beggin
Is the same momma in need
And that old woman saucing sub's
Is the same old hag.
The same ride or die
Is the same house wife
Ain't no differences amongst us
Goddesses of the earth,

the core

the motivators of energy that materialize
So stop making it seem like
The crack head is less than the girl that catches the bus
Or the baby momma is more dramatic than a virgin
We all women dealing with men with the same problems
It's called survival!
I'm tired of the church girl verses the Muslim
The boss chick verses the hood rat
The she did this or she did that let's stay honest we all the same
Each requiring only one thang
Perspective on how to grow!
Damn y'all slow!
We don't care long as the beat slow enough to snap or fingers to

And fast enough to make our booty move
We women
Harriet, and Franklin

Earhart and Baker
Myself and haters
No testosterone
Just sauce, vagina, and gumption

Stop separating us
Dividing us
Lying to us
Tapering us

We be wild and free and prepared to learn from everything
we go through
Every one of us is the divine in every one of us
What we do is just a costume.
Just a costume
Just a costume on repea

6 PART SIX

Brothas

I mean real brothers
Are the shit!

With they funny shaped heads and thick bodies

Man, them ones right there

Have you begging the lords mercy

When he look over the black women's lines
Curvy and wide
Thin and thick
He licks his lips
Them brothas be the shit

The ones who loves black girls

Cuz we down home, nurturing and strong,
Know how to cook when the cookies get low

The ones who love our hair
two days pass after washing,
all tangled,
and sticking straight out

He call it handle bars

And hold on to these coils for dear life

For we are life my dear
We are home, we are whole, we are here

Sistas

I mean Real sisters are the shit…

She loves me like body rubs and hair twists
Like hot baths when my body aches
Like pictures of my pain
And patronage of my art
She love me like caring for my children so that I can pursue my dreams

Like gas money and $30 just because she knows I'm broke

She love me like love supposed to be
Like treating me to dinner when I owe her money

Like forgetting that I owe her money

Like forgiving that I owe her money

We barter truth for loyalty
Love for laughter
No one is ever left empty
Accounts always in the black

Our love is bigger and realer than that

Raw like fresh fruit and new scars

Radiant like full moon fire
Reminiscent of birthing, such a necessary and transformational

aching

Rarer than a Ruby in the Rough

www.ingramcontent.com/pod-product-compliance
Lightning Source LLC
LaVergne TN
LVHW050951080826
845145LV00004B/1464

* 9 7 8 0 5 7 8 5 7 8 4 2 2 *